A Place of Encounter

On Poetry, Teaching, and Faith

Thomas Gardner

HERE BELOW BOOKS
GRAND RAPIDS, MICHIGAN

Here Below Books is an imprint of
Wm. B. Eerdmans Publishing Co.
2006 44th Street SE, Grand Rapids, MI 49508
herebelowbooks.com

Published 2026

Printed in the United States of America

32 31 30 29 28 27 26 1 2 3 4 5 6 7

ISBN 978-0-8028-8596-8

Library of Congress Cataloging-in-Publication Data

A catalog record for this book is available from the Library of Congress.

Permissions to reprint the materials used in this book are acknowledged on pages 137–39.

"*A Place of Encounter* is the testimonial of a great thinker who for decades seems to have thought by teaching, as poets think by writing. And although I have taught for a number of years, reading the book I found it most natural to imagine myself as one of Thomas Gardner's students. It is one of Gardner's gifts that his writing is so engrossing as to make one wish one had spent one's formative years learning from it, and from him."

—**Shane McCrae,** author of
The Many Hundreds of the Scent

"*A Place of Encounter* by Thomas Gardner is a radiant collection of short essays that dwell on the interwoven life of soul and body—the ear receiving the body as lived presence, or as a staged play unfolding in many parts; the incarnational act of reading itself. Gardner traces the interior work of a poet's soul by close-reading a sequence of beloved poems, encountering a vivid menagerie of images: Frost's birches and woods, Heaney's bogs, Bishop's moose and armadillo, Stevens's sea and singing woman, among many others. Through these meditations emerge sacred moments of surprise and wonder, startling turns of phrase, and honest exchanges with his students—priceless moments of human connection, empathy, and slow, luminous revelation."

—**Karen An-hwei Lee,** author of *The Beautiful Immunity* and *Duress*

"Gardner's meditations on a life in and through poetry are like a succession of glasses of the best, cool water on a warm day. As he observes, 'Poems, like parables, ask us to find ourselves within a certain situation, to move a certain way. They don't ask if we understand. They ask us to keep up.' These gentle micro-essays offer a testimony of Gardner's effort to keep up—and offer to walk with the reader, briefly but indelibly."

—**G. C. Waldrep,** author of *The Opening Ritual*

For Edward Weisband

and in memory of Jack Wheatcroft

INTRODUCTION

The poet G. C. Waldrep describes poetry as "a place of encounter" with what he calls "radical otherness." Poetry has many names for this radical otherness: God, the sea, the present moment; silence, possibility, the real. It is not yet spoken, perhaps beyond words, and yet it calls out, seeking to be known. Poetry is a record of that encounter, a mind or a heart shaken, redirected, deepened, and changed. A staging of that encounter. When we read a poem, we are called to reperform that act, working out inwardly, within ourselves, how we might move forward, step by step, on that inward journey. Poems, like parables, ask us to find ourselves within a certain situation, to move a certain way. They don't ask if we understand. They ask us to keep up.

Thought about this way, poems become, the poet Tim Lilburn writes, a means of change, "spiritual exercises by which human beings are lifted and altered, made, that is, more richly human." As we answer their demands, finding within ourselves a way of moving from, for example, a lack of knowing to a reopening of the world, we are doing spiritual work, however we understand it. "For the writer or reader of faith," Waldrep adds, "one's engagement with that work—with any work—is . . . an act of faith. The engagement is itself a sanctuary, a temple, a field of encounter." And this would be true of "any work" because, for a reader of faith, one's relation to the divine is part of what one draws from in doing the work serious poems ask of us, an aspect of one's inner world to be engaged.

Let me give an example from a poem I discuss in one of the short essays that follow: Elizabeth Bishop's "The End of March," a poem not obviously written from a position of faith but that nonetheless can richly engage it. The poem describes a walk on a Massachusetts beach on a cold, windy day. The poet and two friends find themselves in a world in which everything is "withdrawn," "shrunken," "inaudible." An attempt by the poet to tease that world into some sort of meaning ends in a "sodden" snarl of "wet white string," cast aside and unreadable. The poet pauses on her walk, brought to a halt by the cold wind, and describes the "proto-dream-house" she had hoped to lead her friends to—a house she'd fantasized about retiring to and doing "nothing / or nothing much [in], forever." Her language yearns and soars, arching toward what she describes as the house's "heavy with light" perfection, and then breaks off—this is an impossible vision, doubly so on a day such as this. She turns back with her friends, their faces "freezing on the other side," and finds herself caught up in a world of wonder, the shoreline's previously inert details transformed by the momentarily appearing sun into a bejeweled playground of darting, invisible forces.

These details make up the poem's plot, which it is possible to summarize more or less straightforwardly as I have just done. But to "do" the poem, to stage it inwardly, one must also find a way to connect its elements, working out how an initial experience of blankness might lead one to its impossible dream of richness and fullness, and then, more deeply, how turning one's back on that dream might suddenly open one's eyes to a world glinting with everything one had yearned for and been denied. To answer those questions, as I'll demonstrate in the essays that follow, one must unfold these movements within, walking one's own version of that broken beach and its impossible dream and then taking on the gap between this broken world and what one yearns for in such a way that it becomes, as Waldrep suggests, a temple or sanctuary or field of encounter. That acknowledging brokenness and need gives one eyes to see is an insight rooted in faith, however one defines it, and drawing from faith's inner dynamics of need and grace is one way one becomes capable of doing what a poem such as Bishop's calls us to.

In these essays I think back over my forty years of teaching at Virginia Tech and try to describe the spiritual demands and opportunities for growth brought about by reading in this way. I've read poems with students from many different backgrounds and spiritual commitments, who drew on different histories and needs and responded to the poems in quite different ways. Engaging with the poems, which were mostly from the modern and contemporary periods, became for a number of my students an inner spiritual exercise. Getting lost and finding yourself changed—asking how you got there, what you did there, why the body suddenly came alive, what it was like to discover yourself in the words of others—all of that became the work of the class.

The following essays work lyrically, encouraging the reader to join in the experience of wrestling with and being changed by these questions. They do not so much try to survey the work of my classes as to focus on certain particulars of certain poems, convinced that such encounters, as Lilburn puts it, "groove interior change." Most of the poems I refer to are readily available online, and all the titles are listed in the Notes section at the back of the book. I work through four poems in the central sections of the book in detail—Robert Hass's "The Apple Trees at Olema," Elizabeth Bishop's "At the Fishhouses," Jorie Graham's "Fission," and Robert Frost's "The Wood-Pile"—in order to demonstrate how one would go about, in a sustained way, meeting the demands of poems in the life-changing ways they call us to.

That is, after all, what poems have always been about. I've thought for years about the moment in T. S. Eliot's "The Waste Land" in which, near the end of a long movement of the spirit from an acknowledgment of brokenness to the first stirrings of an openness to "the heart of light, the silence," Eliot takes us through an exercise in which he draws from his own heart in articulating the voice calling out to him in his brokenness. Drawing from a portion of the Upanishads, Eliot captures, in the wordless thunder, a voice whose demands could be translated in three different ways—give, sympathize, control—and then, much as we do when we read a poem, works out the implications of these terms within his own spirit. "Give," for example, suggests a way toward life through the giving of alms, and so it has often been read, but Eliot finds his own way there. "What have we given?" he responds, and then attempts an answer:

> My friend, blood shaking my heart
> The awful daring of a moment's surrender
> Which an age of prudence can never retract
> By this, and this only, we have existed.

This confession—that he had once given himself to something or someone other than himself and that, however heart-shaking the implications of that act, he had found in that act life itself—changes him. It moves his spirit forward. So, I'm suggesting, does any (deep) act of reading. Eliot left a record of his reading to encourage us to do likewise, and here, in my own way, I do as well.

PLAY

Some years ago, my friend Patty Raun put on a play based on my poetry classes. She had joined us for a semester and commented that, in breaking a poet's thought into parts and then reenacting it, we were essentially doing theater. Could we try it on the stage?

I wasn't sure how to begin. I wrote out a monologue, working through five or six of my favorite poems, and Patty held auditions, gathered actors, and began reading my words out loud to herself at night. Eventually, she said, she began hearing two different ways of speaking. She gave one set of lines to the most verbally gifted actor—a woman named Leah—and the other set to a group of eight who became a kind of chorus, or, as we later came to think of them, Leah's body.

We called the play *Ear, and I, and Silence*, after an Emily Dickinson line. Center stage, Leah would bring up a poem, break it into sections, and begin leading us through what she saw there. The chorus would gather about her, informally at first, in ones and twos, listen to her observations, and then begin extending them, balancing one thought against another, slowing them down and reimagining them as movement in space. They were bringing Leah's thought to life, and as we watched from the audience, she would edge close to one group and then another, yearning to be part of it all, her words deepened and changed, turned about within the unfolding dance.

I still remember the soreness in my hands the nights the play ran, clutching the railing in front of me, my voice doubling back on itself, spotlit and heightened, no longer mine alone. I felt as if I was outside of myself, all of us together, actors and audience, alive in the dark, moving as one through space.

ACT OF FINDING

I had, by then, begun to focus my classes on Wallace Stevens's description of poetry as a mind in action, "the mind in the act of finding / What will suffice," not declaring something it already knows but, in some uncharted space, working its way toward it. Just as we did in class, Leah and the chorus were reperforming that act of finding, walking through a series of poems.

Stevens pictures a darkened theater and the poet "like an insatiable actor, slowly and / With meditation, speak[ing] words that in the ear, / In the delicatest ear of the mind, repeat, / Exactly, that which it wants to hear." Those lines have always intrigued me. Stevens's poet is alone on a stage, listening to himself speak, guided by what the ear of his mind, that "delicatest ear," most wants to hear—its inner contours formed and shaped and given expression. "Twanging an instrument, twanging a wiry string," he makes his way down its passages, inviting what he calls the poem's "invisible audience" into that music, listening "not to the play, but to itself, expressed / In an emotion as of two people, as of two / Emotions becoming one." What we were transfixed by, there in the dark, was the work of reading, Leah and the chorus coming together and pulling apart, "becoming one" with the emotion they were unfolding, drawing upon their own inner histories in bringing the poems' music to light.

CHAIN

I remember driving across the country with my brother John, years ago. He was at the wheel and, as often happened, doing most of the talking. It was dark, and I remember feeling, as we slipped through space, that we were sharing one voice, circling, probing, coming to a halt, something unsaid between us being drawn to the surface. Kenneth Burke describes a similar coming together as the reader reperforms the "symbolic act" of a poem, linking action to action in an improvised inward chain. I miss my brother. He's been dead for ten years, and that night in the car was almost fifty years ago. But those long, downhill curves, our bodies shifting back and forth, that shared, endless reaching—I can go there still. That, it seems to me, is what

Leah and the chorus were enacting on stage —our attempt, day after day, to access, in our reading, a rising music, tracing back to its source our shared fragility, uncovering there a home.

BODY

Whitman called that inner ear the soul. "Loafe with me on the grass," he wrote. "Loose the stop from your throat, / Not words, not music or rhyme I want, not custom or lecture, not even the best, / Only the lull I like, the hum of your valvèd voice." In calling the soul to the body, Whitman was calling it to itself. "I mind how once we lay such a transparent summer morning," he whispers. "How you settled your head athwart my hips and gently turn'd over upon me, / And parted the shirt from my bosom-bone, and plunged your tongue to my bare-stript heart." That invitation is what the soul most wants to hear—sweeping it up, by means of the body's charged vulnerability, into a “knowledge / . . . pass[ing] all the argument of the earth.”

This was always the best part of teaching for me, that rising “hum” as our bodies unfolded, along with the poet, the motions of the soul. The body undefended, hair still wet —I usually ran before I taught—reaching, failing, rising beyond itself.

Let’s start there. Why was that so important? What were those years of teaching all about?

TOUCH

"All we can offer is our human fragility," my friend Edward once wrote to me, following up on a long conversation we had had about teaching one summer. He had read some work of mine and remarked on how often I had turned to the words *as if*, calling attention to the vulnerability behind that acknowledgment of not-knowing. He saw it as an act of faith, a giving of myself over to the improvisatory nature of making.

When the shootings occurred at Virginia Tech in 2007, classes were canceled for ten days. When they began again, I remember the great relief I felt on returning to my Whitman/Dickinson class and realizing, after days of repeating to one another "There are no words for this," that this particular class did in fact have the words. We had already enacted them, trusting them with our weight. "I felt a Funeral, in my Brain, / And Mourners to and fro / Kept treading —treading—till it seemed / That Sense was breaking through—" one of my students began, trying to describe, in those first days, how our minds kept circling and circling what we couldn't accept, stepping with Dickinson from plank to plank above that uncertain abyss.

When classes began again, Edward worked his way up and down the rows of his political science lecture class—perhaps 150 students, my wife told me; she had been assigned as a counselor to that room and simply stood silently in the back and watched—greeting and touching each student, looking them in the eyes and asking how they were doing, offering, as Dickinson had, his own fragility as a space in which to dwell.

DASH

One of the pieces we staged was Elizabeth Bishop's "Poem," a poem I love and have carried with me for years. Bishop describes a small painting given to her by relatives that no one had really looked at. "It must be Nova Scotia," she begins, taking the scene in and moving back and forth between bits of paint and what they represent, lifting up each element and piecing them together as houses, a church, a meadow, exactly as we did in class with words. Leah worked this out with a delicate, knowing precision, getting a bit of a laugh when she couldn't distinguish a flyspeck from a bird, and then she stopped. "Heavens, I recognize the place," she continued, voicing the poem. "I know it! / It's behind—I can almost remember the farmer's name," the last words almost stuttered out. It wasn't just Nova Scotia—it was a scene from Bishop's own childhood.

And here the chorus took over, their unfolding chain of shoulders and backs leading her down through that open space:

> It's behind—I can almost remember
>   the farmer's name.
> His barn backed on that meadow.
>   There it is,
> titanium white, one dab.

I love the space of that dash. Turning for a moment away from the painting, Leah paused and focused her eyes on the meadow in her mind, working her way down its length until she found the barn, found it in herself, and then, the barn alive in her mind, turned back to the painting and found it there as well: "titanium white, one dab." Whenever I teach this poem, I find myself moving my shoulders as I try to find a way to say this. What had been a dab of paint became for Bishop part of a living world. That dash was where the work got done.

I almost never forget a landscape. Decades later, driving down a road I had once been on, I'll be able to sense, just before we round a bend, the configuration of fields and fog rising up to meet us. It's as if I had looked ahead within myself. So too in class. Much of what we did, in getting the details of a poem right, was setting up a space for that moment of recognition to occur—the moment when we saw, as if around a bend, the temptation or problem the poet was making her way through. The landscape. We would each then go there in ourselves, working our bodies through its pauses and turns until the details of the poem, its dabs of paint, rose before us as living things.

Bishop calls that an act of grace, "the little we get for free," "our two looks," the poet's and the reader's, coming together in a habitable space, "about the size of our abidance." Poems return us to ourselves. "There it is," we say, as if, in reading, we had been read by the poem.

LOST

Thoreau visualized the space of the dash as a landscape after a snowstorm, where the soul awakens to the strangeness of the world:

> In our most trivial walks, we are constantly, though unconsciously, steering like pilots by certain well-known beacons and headlands, and if we go beyond our usual course we still carry in our minds the bearing of some neighboring cape; and not till we are completely lost, or turned around,—for a man needs only to be turned round once with his eyes shut in the world to be lost,—do we appreciate the vastness and strangeness of Nature. Every man has to learn the points of compass again

> as often as he awakes, whether from sleep or any abstraction. Not till we are lost, in other words, not till we have lost the world, do we begin to find ourselves, and realize where we are and the infinite extent of our relations.

You must die in order to live, Jesus says in the words behind this passage, for it is in losing that we are found, awakening to a vastness not yet marked or unfolded.

This is where we did our work. Dickinson called it "Possibility— / A fairer House than Prose," imagining us there "spreading wide [our] narrow Hands / to gather Paradise." Paradise for Dickinson is what slips through our narrow hands, Thoreau's "infinite . . . relations" discovered as our hands are forced wide.

Poems pose spiritual problems. They turn us around. As Frost puts it, echoing this passage in Thoreau, getting lost is a poem's "directive," what its instructions are designed to accomplish:

> And if you're lost enough to find yourself
> By now, pull in your ladder road behind you

> And put a sign up CLOSED to all but me.
> Then make yourself at home.

Making yourself at home would seem to be solitary work, each of us, in our own way, charting a path alongside the poet. But in doing so, I remember, we inevitably became a "we." I need to think more about this.

NOTE

I had a student once who, after we did that great Stevens poem "The Snow Man," left class, scribbled a note to her roommate about developing "a mind of winter," and went off to the woods to "do" the poem, seeking to become so cold that, as the poem whispered, "nothing [her]self," she might sense the presence of "nothing that is not there and the nothing that is." Imagine her hat and coat alongside the trail, the wind in the trees rising and falling, the self dissolving in a flurry of white. She kept the note and showed it to me years later when our poetry play opened. She was in many ways the inspiration behind Leah.

Blue pen, open hand, a hint of unease—I wondered if I had crossed a line those years before. I can still see myself in class unfolding the poem and, for several moments, not being able to move. Kylie had followed me out there. Curtains of white, the biting cold. In those few moments, standing stock-still, it was as if I was experiencing the poem for the first time, though I'd taught it by then many times before.

PAUSE

A friend showed me how to hear a poem in its pauses. We were in a restaurant, talking about "Prufrock." I had never really understood the end of the poem with its mermaids and white hair blown back. It seemed trivial somehow, and my friend insisted that I had hurried through the stanza breaks where the real thinking of the poem takes place. "I have heard the mermaids singing, each to each" isn't resigned, she said, not quite, although it's only in looking back that Prufrock can find them. But then there's a pause, a break in which he must have turned in on his own empty heart and burst out, in utter exhaustion, "I do not think that they will sing to me." Not now, not ever. A second pause. Can you do that? she asked. Can you find your way there? Listen, she said, and I did, everyone did, as out of that pause a second thought arose, defiantly, out of death: "I have *seen* them riding seaward on the waves / Combing the white hair of the waves blown back." Just at the moment Prufrock acknowledges its passing, he sees that other world. In not possessing it, he comes near. Every eye in the restaurant was on us.

I had another student, on the second day of class, who came up to me in tears. We had worked our way through these lines, and something in them had come too close. She felt exposed, violated, as if a piece of her had been brought to the surface and handed around. Hadn't I noticed? Hadn't everyone? Listen, I said. What do you hear? It wasn't about the rest of the class. The space between us now so deeply charged that everyone else had vanished.

PERMISSION

Fifty years ago, when I was a student at Bucknell, running cross-country and track for Art Gulden and cobbling together an English major after failing to make it as a chemical engineer, I ran into Jack Wheatcroft near the library. I had taken his two courses on the British novel and had fallen in love with the way he thought, straining for something just out of reach before coming to a halt and staring out a classroom window. He stopped me and congratulated me on doing well in the Penn Relays marathon the previous week. He had seen the results in the paper—*The New York Times*, I think, or perhaps *The Philadelphia Inquirer*. I was floored, first, that he recognized me outside of class, and second, that an English professor read the sports pages. I had worked quite hard at walling off the various parts of my life from each other, and here was someone I deeply admired casually bringing them together. A few years before he died, when I reminded Jack of this conversation, he told me that, having grown up in Philadelphia, he knew all about the Penn Relays. Of course he followed the results. That moment stayed with me, beginning the process of dissolving the walls between thinking and my body, daily work and what would become my spiritual life, freeing each realm to speak into the other.

That's the space poetry leads us to. And over the years, I would offer students bits of my story, as I'm doing now, sliding one landscape up against another, chipping away at those inner walls and inviting more of ourselves in. It was for freedom Christ set us free, and the classroom was perhaps the primary space I most felt this in play. But you have to pay attention. I remember whole poems, at some student's chance remark, opening up an entirely unlooked for range of reference, suddenly lifting into visibility, like the ridges on fall mornings east of my house shaking off the nighttime's fog.

HAIR

I often think about a scene in Terrence Malick's *The Tree of Life* in which Jack O'Brien, working his way through a midlife crisis, tries to understand how his mother survived the sudden death of his brother. He imagines the moment she and his father first got the news. They're inconsolable, adrift in a series of empty rooms and frozen tableaux, and we see Jack as an adult, years after the fact, enter the scene, touch his mother's hair, and look up at her face in her grief. He's not there, of course, but he is somehow, improvising, with his body, a doorway into her emptiness. Attending to it. How was she not destroyed? he asks.

That was our question after the shootings, as Dickinson's "I felt a Funeral" accompanied us downward. Striving to make sense, going numb, being overwhelmed, finally falling, outside the bounds of reason —we used our own histories to find a way through the stages of Dickinson's collapse, all but touching her hair, "hit[ting] a World, at every plunge." We knew she had survived. There must be some way through in which it was not only loss that greeted us as we "finished knowing—then—."

CHANGED

A while back, I received an email from a student describing the day, maybe fifteen years ago, we read Stevens's "The Idea of Order at Key West" and the way something had come loose inside him as the woman in that poem embraced, as he put it, "the whole confluence of scene and sea" before her, neither interpreting the sea nor echoing it back, simply, in her singing, making a home in its tensions. "That moment still here," he wrote: "the moment of question, or confusion, or potential, whatever it was. And how you sort of stirred at things (your fingers would branch out as you gestured, like you'd become whisk-handed), gathering ideas, neither discounting nor allowing us to finalize whatever it was we were doing, together, as a class. Multiple options, alive in the moment. How as we worked toward the ending, trying to square what we felt now with what we'd felt before, we understood that we had been changed."

It's hard to see yourself from the outside, but this rings true. Jorie Graham calls it an act of faith, this giving yourself to the moment, undergoing it. "This is the force of faith," she writes. "Nobody gets / what they want. Never again are you the same. The longing / is to be pure. What you get is to be changed." Weston was surely remembering these lines—what you get is to be changed.

BACKWARDS

We would sometimes use the term "backwards" from Elizabeth Bishop's "The Man-Moth" to talk about what it was like to move through those empty spaces. Bishop comes on that word late in her poem. She has invented a creature, half man, half moth, who scales buildings at night, drawn toward the light of the moon. "He thinks the moon is a small hole at the top of the sky, / proving the sky quite useless for protection," but "must investigate as high as he can climb." He fails to make his way through, of course, and when he returns to his home in the subway, he seats himself "facing the wrong way," turning his back on what lies ahead. The train, from that position, seems to start "at once at its full, terrible speed, / without a shift in gears or a gradation of any sort. / He cannot tell the rate at which he travels backwards." Acknowledging the hole in the sky leads him to turn his back on the world, exposing himself to its terrible speed, taking it on in his body. Unguarded, lurching, achingly self-aware, he keeps his hands in his pockets to ward off the temptation of the third rail.

This is the position we read and write from, Bishop seems to suggest. If you catch the man-moth and pay attention, you might see "one tear, his only possession," slip from an eye. If you continue to watch, "he'll hand it over, / cool as from underground springs and pure enough to drink." That tear is inwardness itself, pure enough to drink, quivering with the soul's valved voice. It's why we come to poems. There doesn't seem to be a choice: You either know there's a hole in the sky or you don't. But you do get to choose how to seat yourself within that knowing, the lights of the station flaring and falling away, more to the world than you had ever imagined.

GIFT

I had a student once who, after we had worked through "The Man-Moth," came up after class and asked if I could say more about being backwards. I had asked about the holes in our own skies, and the floodgates had opened, each of us grappling with the awareness that, at some level, the fundamentals of our lives, unthinkingly trusted in, were in fact "quite useless for protection." We all understood that, having acknowledged such a thing, the trains we returned to—the self, the body, language itself—would be forever different. But why, he seemed to be asking, would you deliberately go there? I went over the poem again, but as he walked away, I knew I hadn't answered his question. His eyes that couldn't meet mine. The two of us together in the empty room, its borders and edges having come undone. "I understand" was the best I could manage, but I didn't, really. I didn't know what sort of hole had opened up within him, but clearly he hadn't asked for it. There is work to be done there, I wish I had said. Inner work. He had been given a gift, but I didn't know yet how to say that.

CHARGED

When the world turns you backwards, your body comes alive. That would have been a place to start. Think of the beginning of "The Wood-Pile," where Frost's speaker, "out walking in the frozen swamp one gray day," pauses before going further on, his body awakened by the blankness he's about to enter. We had done that poem together the year before. "The hard snow held me, save where now and then / One foot went through," Frost writes, the four beats of "hard snow held me" skittering off into "save where now and then." The world is no longer solid. Imagine missing a stair in the dark and your momentum carrying you forward and down—that flash of alertness. You don't see this in your mind as much as you do it with your body, finding in those lines the charged vulnerability you'll need to follow the poet into the unknown. You've felt that driving on ice, haven't you?—that first slip when you lose contact with the road, alive inside as you continue on, the world flaring and scattering against your windshield.

VULNERABLE

Graham describes that feeling as "vertigo." In one poem, she pictures herself on the edge of a cliff, taking the world in and then sensing it slide away. She's backwards to her footing, "the mind trying to fasten / and fasten, the mind feeling it like a sickness this wanting / to snag, catch hold, begin, the mind crawling out to the edge of the cliff / and feeling the body as if for the first time—how it cannot / follow, cannot love." I've always wondered, as the body comes alive here, why it insists on what it cannot do. I asked about this the last time I taught the poem, and one of my students wrote to me, later that night, as if from the edge of that very cliff: "It's the feeling of being vulnerable, there at the edge. You raise your hand and you're about to get called on. Your heart rate increases, your breath quickens and becomes shallow, and you start to sweat. It's a physical reaction. You become more than just a mind with thoughts. You find yourself whole again, this weird, wonderful body a part of who you are and how you process the world."

I think that's right. Our fragile bodies —sweaty and alert, deep in the grip of what can't be possessed, cannot follow, cannot love, and yet, caught up in a multiplicity they can never sort out—understand it in a way the mind, with its single focus, never can. The world comes alive. How vast and strange it all seems, how much we would give to embrace it.

SLIP

Bishop called that feeling "strangeness." She discovered it embedded in the most ordinary of moments—walking a beach, slipping through the night on a bus, skimming a magazine in a waiting room, the familiar world slipping away and "a peripheral vision of whatever it is one can never really see full-face but that seems enormously important" rising in its place. She was writing about Darwin: "One admires the beautiful, solid case being built up out of his endless heroic *observations*, almost unconscious or automatic—and then comes a sudden relaxation, a forgetful phrase, and one *feels* the strangeness of his undertaking, sees the lonely young man, his eyes fixed on facts and minute details, sinking or sliding giddily off into the unknown." She was, of course, also talking about her own work, how the mind, in her poems, concentrating, concentrating, would suddenly relax, its borders of attention giving way before an open-ended blankness.

One does feel giddy there. I always loved those moments when my students would clutch their heads and pillow their chins and grow silent, their eyes fixed elsewhere, as if we had worked our way in so deep that nothing remained but concentration itself. Bishop calls this a "self-forgetful, perfectly useless concentration." Sometimes when I run, I forget I am anchored to the ground and drift above it for a few steps, outside the body, outside of words, backwards to them both. I might have returned to that, with my "backwards" student, that self-forgetful, perfectly useless concentration.

HUM

A few years ago, after church, a friend asked me to pray for her daughter who'd just had a miscarriage. We drew our chairs together in the back of the sanctuary. I began to pray and, after a moment, Donna began to hum, in time with my words but outside of their worried indirection and brief stabs at comfort, not wishing the sadness away so much as moving freely within it. Grief sifted through her like shadows across a landscape. It was as if she had heard an opening in my words and gone there.

I loved, in class, those moments when, in the midst of our careful stitchwork, idea to idea and image to image, something quickened, a glance or phrase snatched from the air and improvised on, the room, as it seemed, beginning to hum, a wave of arousal rising through us as if we were a single body. A friend recently sent me a clip from Scorsese's *No Direction Home*. It was of a crowded room and Bob Dylan composing —typing, swaying, using his body to sound out the soul. That loose-limbed focus. Joan Baez, over his shoulder, quietly sang one of his songs, and Dylan, without ever moving his eyes, reached back to where he had once been and brought that energy forward, the whole room beginning to hum. I often thought students heard something in my words that I couldn't hear myself—perhaps it's always this way—as, unmoored, they found a new way to their footing.

IMPROVISE

When my daughters were young—this is now more than thirty years ago—I would sometimes take them out in the car, drive some distance away from town, and then begin asking them at each intersection to decide which way to turn. This might go on for an hour, maybe more, and it must have seemed to them as if we were thoroughly lost, though I'd nudge us, now and again, back on a way that would take us home. It was a blast, charged, a little scary. With each new choice, I'd have to reimagine how to get home. Time itself seemed to open and stand still, lit up from within in the mock-desperate hilarity of the car.

I felt something like that most days in class. I would take us through poems by asking questions, linking part to part but allowing what my students noticed to turn the discussion and redirect us, my own inner map continually redrawn by how they responded, uncertainty part of the awakening. I knew the landscape, of course, how it held together, but what I didn't know was what would rise in me as I listened to my students think, the confusions and possibilities at each new crossroad. I was improvising, of course—all of us were—backwards at times to thinking itself but making a way, tracing a music deeper and more unexpected than any of us could hear alone.

LINE

At one point in *Walden*, Thoreau describes returning to the woods after an evening in town and going out on the pond to fish. It's midnight, moonlit, and he's serenaded by owls and foxes and the creaking note of an unknown bird. He drops an anchor and finds himself "surrounded by thousands of small perch and shiners, dimpling the surface with their tails in the moonlight," but he soon turns his attention below, "communicating by a long flaxen line with mysterious nocturnal fishes that had their dwelling forty feet below, or sometimes dragging sixty feet of line about the pond as I drifted in the gentle night breeze, now and then feeling a slight vibration along it, indicative of some life prowling about the extremity." Imagine his hand, light on the line, taking in what he cannot see.

As we talked through poems, I wasn't just interested in information, although getting the details right mattered. I was waiting for a phrase that might take us deeper. Repeating back what I heard, I would rest my hands on my students' words, waiting for something there to vibrate. I'd get shivers when it brushed by below us. I never knew what might be said or how I might use it. Sometimes I would gather up two or three comments before, resting my hands on them, I'd suddenly see how the space between them might be mapped. Thoreau describes fishing in two realms at once: in the pond and in the heavens. It was a matter of trust on my students' part, venturing forth a line of words and waiting to see where it might lead. Thousands of small fish, dimpling the surface in the moonlight.

HANDS

There were days, as we worked through poems, that our boundaries would begin to slip. We would have no real sense, after a while, of who was responsible for each new insight, who was touching whom. There's an extraordinary passage in *Moby-Dick* in which Ishmael describes sitting with a group of sailors, hands in a vat of cooling and about-to-crystalize spermaceti, squeezing the just-forming globules back into liquid so it could be processed. He describes a near-erotic "insanity" as he loses track of his hands deep in the "inexpressible." "I found myself unwittingly squeezing my co-laborers' hands in it, mistaking their hands for the gentle globules," he writes, "squeez[ing] ourselves into each other." This is a kind of thinking done with the hands, he writes, driven not by "the intellect or the fancy" but by savoring the textures accessed by touch—"the wife, the heart, the bed, the table, the saddle, the fireside, the country"—making a new sort of home there.

Leaving the poem open as long as we did—squeezing it, keeping it fluid—was how we released its life. That's why lecturing always seemed so flat to me—thinking with no one else to brush against or lean upon. Many days I would leave class unable to say how we had gotten to where we ended up, though I knew it when we arrived. The very play of the hour's dynamics, using and losing and blending our voices, seemed to open a space alongside the poem where, if I could somehow circle back to it, I could still trace how we had moved before it was covered over by falling snow.

MORNING

Some time ago, reading Robert Hass's *The Apple Trees at Olema*, I began to notice how many of his poems begin with the notation "this morning," in various forms: "The light this morning is touching everything"; "On the morning of the Käthe Kollwitz exhibit"; "Mornings on the south side of the house / just outside the kitchen door / arrived early in summer—." I love that time of day as well —the light, the smells, the first moments of attention—but Hass was responding to more than that. "Morning is when I am awake and there is a dawn in me," writes Thoreau. Standing in that first light, giving himself to it as an act of faith, Hass was opening himself to an inner dawn, expecting something to be drawn into visibility there in that moment. Closing the door and going through notes I had scrawled on the board of where we had been the previous class was my way of saying "this morning," throwing off sleep and putting us into a position where the light might once again strike us. Those notes were only marginally readable, but I knew we needed something to push off from, something to leave behind.

HOUSE

On their fifty-third anniversary, my father hatched a plan in which he would write a letter to my mother each morning for a year, recounting their history together. She was sixteen and he was eighteen when they met. And he did it, 366 letters, small loose-leaf pages kept in a notebook, which he passed on to me last year. It's a fascinating journey: nineteen houses in five states, five children, a lie he told in graduate school to break free of an overzealous adviser, a certain restlessness never quite at home, never sure how long any move might last. Through it all, you can sense the presence of my mother, still sleeping while he re-created their world. The thought of her was as much the point of each letter as the remembered details. It was as if my father had paused their marriage and entered it backwards, still half asleep, the night's restlessness poured into each day's writing. I can see him moving through those houses, inhabiting each in turn, touching in my mother's conjured company something he could never reach alone.

Class was that way too. As we performed our poems, furnishing and pacing out their rooms, desire was leading us on, stretching toward something just out of reach. We were caught up in an intimacy we had been fathered and mothered by. Children will "speak our speech and never know," Wallace Stevens writes of the words we leave behind—bones on a hillside, shadows across a roofline. What a privilege, in my memories of class as in those letters, to catch a glimpse of what Stevens calls "the look of things," the very ribs of our world falling into place as we took up the words that had formed it.

AS IF

Over my desk, I have a photo of the house Virginia Woolf's family rented in St. Ives the summers before her mother died. It looks up from the garden at the empty drawing room steps where Mrs. Ramsay had been reading to James in *To the Lighthouse*, the scene Lily Briscoe tried to paint in the beginning of the book and, ten years later, after Mrs. Ramsay's death and the undoing of the family, returned to again at its close. She had loved Mrs. Ramsay and was trying to "express that emptiness there, . . . one's body feeling [it], not one's mind, . . . to want and want and not to have." Her brush begins to move again within that loss, wrestling with what she calls life's central question, embodied for her there, which had always evaded her.

In "Spring Drawing," struggling with another sort of loss and, like Lily, unable to "find his way to a sentence" capable of resolving it, Robert Hass discovers, in the act of thinking, a tumbling series of "as ifs" cascading from that failure, creating what he calls "habitable space, lived in beyond wishing." He was surely thinking of these last pages in Woolf in which, as Lily stares at those empty steps, a bit of white catches her eye and, brush in hand, the blurred painting becoming "clear for a second, she drew a line there, in the centre," bringing that emptiness into focus. *As if*, in the Hass poem, is not a way of bridging the gap between what we have and what we yearn for but, much like my students' prefacing each response with "I'm not sure, but," a way of feeling one's way through the gap's empty space, embodying in the simplest of verbal gestures what Hass calls, nodding to Woolf, "the energy of *brush* and *stroke*."

ATTUNED

Before I fell in love with Bishop and Hass, I found myself obsessed with a series of extraordinary paragraphs in Marilynne Robinson's novel *Housekeeping*. I think of this as the first real poetry I read on my own. I pulled it off a bookstore shelf in graduate school in 1980 and have returned to it many times, copying out certain passages over and over in an attempt to work out their music. In the novel, the narrator, Ruth, looks back on her childhood, focusing on the crucial years after she lost her mother and grandmother and was raised, with her sister, by their eccentric Aunt Sylvie, a drifter who, even after settling down, "kept house" by opening it to "the very element[s] it was made to exclude." Sylvie, Ruth remembers, "liked to eat supper in the dark," gathering the girls "just when the windows went stark blue" and seating them before a radiance as "luminous and cool as aquarium glass and as warped as water," the world beyond pouring in through the now-erased windows, filling the house to an unaccountable depth. "Sylvie talked a great deal about housekeeping," Ruth remarks, but it was housekeeping of a peculiar sort, involving strong solvents, open air, and a deliberate refusal to disturb the "Delphic niceness" of the leaves and scraps of paper that had drifted into the corners of the house:

> Every time a door was opened anywhere in the house there was a sound from all the corners of lifting and alighting. I noticed that the leaves would be lifted up by something that came before the wind, they would tack against some impalpable movement of air several seconds before the wind was heard in the trees. Thus finely did our house become attuned to the

orchard and to the particularities of weather, even in the first days of Sylvie's housekeeping.

I came to think of Ruth's prose as a version of her aunt's housekeeping. It seats itself backwards to the ordinary, opening itself to an uncertainty we would normally turn away from and, in embracing that, makes a home, attuned to the "impalpable movement" of spirit just at the edge of consciousness. I would sometimes think of Sylvie as we gathered in class over our reading. Just as she lived for the moment when the house's "stark blue windows" disappeared and the world outside the windows drew close, so we, in tracing out the music of our poems, the fixed boundaries of time and space and distance melting away, found ourselves in velvet night, the air cool to our touch, rushing in.

SPIRIT

One of the passages I kept returning to in my notebooks was Ruth's meditation on her grandmother's loneliness after the death of her husband, traced out in a scene that took place years before Ruth was born. "One day my grandmother must have carried out a basket of sheets to hang in the spring sunlight, in her widow's black," she begins. "*Say* there were two or three inches of hard old snow on the ground, . . . and *say* that when she had pinned three corners to the lines [a sheet] began to billow and leap in her hands, to flare and tremble . . . as if a spirit were dancing in its cerements."

Ruth's *say* is her version of *as if*, reaching into their shared loneliness, touching what she finds there, the word attuned, in its tentative formulations, to the moving spirit dancing in the sheets on the line. The rising wind of her lonely soul—once accessed and put into words—that wind leads Ruth to her grandfather's "serious, mystical excitement" on gusting spring days and his forgetfulness of her grandmother then, which, not surprisingly, was when "she loved him best, as a soul all unaccompanied, like her own." This in turn leads Ruth to the "familiar strangeness" of the summer evenings the spring wind had been announcing and then to the "old women she had known, first her grandmother and then her mother, [who] rocked on their porches in the evenings and sang sad songs, and did not wish to be spoken to." And that strangeness once again returns Ruth to her grandmother, raising three daughters on her own, who, she now sees, would have been granted, in their "unconsciousness" of her, access to a "calm inwardness" they never thought to screen from her sight. "What was it like," she asks of that attunement. One evening her grandmother must have walked out into the garden, savoring her aloneness, Ruth writes. She would have felt "her hair lifted from her neck by a swift, watery wind, and [seen] the trees fill with wind and heard their trunks creak like masts. She [would have] burrowed her hand under a potato plant and felt gingerly for the new potatoes in their dry net of roots, smooth as eggs," whispering as she walked back to the house, her apron full: "What have I seen, what have I seen. The earth and the sky and the garden, not as they always are, . . . quiet and aloof and watchful, so as not to startle the strangeness away."

The flow of Ruth's thought through these paragraphs, the wind of the spirit, caught up in her words, leading her from spring sheets to a position of privileged insight, became for me the music of poetry, making its way through the things of this world. Reproducing its movement as I copied out these passages, I would find my soul lifted into speech, my own loneliness becoming the ground of a deeper knowing. I knew when I began to teach that it was this wind I wanted to channel, but how to go about that?

POISE

That's why Robert Frost was at first so important to me. He taught me to use my body in thinking, giving me something tangible I could actually pass on. For years, early in the semester, I would invite students to try to imagine the deft way, as he puts it in "Birches," thinking about language, he "kept his poise / To the top branches, climbing carefully / With the same pains you use to fill a cup / Up to the brim, and even above the brim," before "he flung outward, feet first, with a swish, / Kicking his way down through the air to the ground," pushing his words to the point of collapse and then riding their collapsing down.

Take "The Wood-Pile," I would say, the way the mind moves there, taking on the open space of a frozen swamp with a series of *as ifs* that, like his footsteps, hold for a moment and then give way. Can you do that? I would ask. The poet steadies himself by taking note of the trees he passes, but finding them "too much alike to mark or name a place by," he turns to a bird, who, he speculates, must think he is pursuing him for his white tail feather, only to inadvertently acknowledge that he is the one doing what he charges the bird with: taking "everything said as personal to himself." He loses his footing over and over, which is why, when he finally comes upon a solidly built woodpile ("four by four by eight") and greets it as everything he had desired, we turn with him and embrace this welcome place of rest. But this too gives way, a dissolution we experience in slow motion if we take the poem in at the speed it demands. There are no tracks in the snow, he notices, so no one has visited it lately. "It was older sure than this year's cutting, / Or even last year's or the year's before," he adds, which would mean it's been abandoned. In fact, we see, as we come closer, all that keeps it upright are the vines wound round it and "a stake and prop, / These latter about to fall." The slow-stepping poise here is extraordinary, and as we rest our weight on each observation, we feel each, in turn, give way, learning never to put our full weight on any one step and arriving at a sort of ever-vigilant acknowledgment of the openness of the world.

Frost concludes the poem with one last attempt at order, imagining a woodcutter who, delighting in "fresh tasks," must have simply forgotten his handiwork and left it behind, "to warm the frozen swamp as best it could / With the slow smokeless burning of decay." All of us in class understood, of course, that at some level that smokeless decay warmed nothing at all, but we had become capable, in taking in the poem at the speed it demanded, of making and unmaking even this final point of rest, balancing both in the same breath.

Poise. I can still remember spreading my fingers as I held myself there, riding "down through the air to the ground."

PLUNGE

I was, for a long time, deeply invested in this vision of pulling back just at the brink of plunging in, turning away but not without a long, deep taste. I loved the resigned beauty of those gestures, the siren call of those dark and empty fields. I had a friend, in my early years of teaching, who would come by and tease me about the end of "Design," that frightening little poem in which Frost speculates that the scene he had stumbled on one morning—a snow-drop spider holding a dead white moth on an unaccountably white flower—must have been pieced together just for him by a force he calls "darkness," seeking to "appall." I heard the poem's last line, out of the open dash ("— / If design govern in a thing so small"), as a delicate turning away from that dark thought. Emphasize the word *if*, I would say to my friend Wyatt, and you can hear Frost shrugging off that nightmare by questioning whether it could actually be in play on such a small scale, reducing the poem to something merely considered, a speculation that might have bruised the speaker but ultimately released him from its grip. My friend would read the line back with a nonexistent ellipsis at the end: "If design govern in a thing so small . . . ," his emphasis falling on *small*. That's not how it ends, I would say, but Wyatt heard what he heard, mocking what he saw as my too-cautious clinging to the edge with a make-believe, haunted-house voice. The reality of the plunge Frost skirted and swerved away from was tangible for me in a way it wasn't for Wyatt—he was fooling around, I wasn't—but Wyatt planted a thought I couldn't let go of. What *would* it be like to never make it back to firmer ground?

TURN

It was finally my students who convinced me that Frost's poise is a bit contrived. Take "Desert Places." Frost begins the poem in motion, "looking into" the blank space of a field he's "going past." That field is the hole in his sky. Night and snow are falling, with "but a few weeds and stubble showing last." The speaker claims to have passed the field, but we can feel it tug him back. The woods on three sides "have" the field, the animals within are "smothered in their lairs," and he is so "absent-spirited" that the empty space he has now returned to sweeps him in, "unawares." I could never do these lines without pacing, glancing back over my shoulder at the field before stopping and gathering myself. In a flurry of nearly identical syllables, almost below the level of words, Frost descends into what we knew had all along had hold of him:

> And lonely as it is, that loneliness
> Will be more lonely ere it will be less—.

The snow and night will continue on, erasing even the weed and stubble we began the poem with, leaving only "a blanker whiteness of benighted snow / With no expression, nothing to express."

That's what the lines mean, but what we felt, doing them with our bodies, was that Frost was speaking not just about the blank field's snow-covered loneliness but about his own. "No expression, nothing to express"—I would want to pause there and let the full weight of that silence take hold, but the poem would begin moving again without us. My students hated that. At the very moment we slowed and were rendered wordless, something in the poem began to fight against itself. "They cannot scare me with their empty spaces / Between stars—on stars where no human race is," he asserts, the *they* giving him something tangible to push off against. "I have it in me so much nearer home / To scare myself with my own desert places," he concludes, as if it had all been a game and he had just been scaring himself. This is surely bluster, I would argue. Frost knows what's pressing in on all sides. He wants us to feel that threat. But my students would have none of that. What they wanted was someone who wouldn't turn away, who might teach them how to live there. They wanted Job and not his friends. They wanted to be brought to their knees and silenced. They knew what it would take to be changed.

YES

Which is where Bishop comes in. Where Frost would let himself be pulled under by the swamp's dark tug and then fight his way back to the surface, Bishop simply lets herself go. Imagine rubbing the back of your hand over a beloved fabric and then drifting off into sleep, the dark quietly drawing you in. Bishop felt as casual as this. I heard this first in her last book, *Geography III*, and then found my way to it in her earlier poems. I remember when "The Moose" came out in *The New Yorker* and not knowing at first what to do with the poem—that long turn away from the familiar ("Goodbye to the elms, / to the farm, to the dog") as the bus journeys west, into the dark, away from home, "moonlight and mist" caught in the woods "like lamb's wool / on bushes in a pasture," the rhythm of the wheels leading us into a "dreamy divagation" in which "a gentle, auditory, / slow hallucination . . ." takes over. The poem pauses at that ellipsis, runs its hand over its surface, and listens.

I began to understand the poem when I relaxed and allowed it to have its way. Imagine the sounds of "Grandparents' voices // uninterruptedly / talking, in Eternity," back in the bus, she instructs us. You can only half hear the words, but the rhythm is clear, one voice and then another, looking back over their lives and responding to the textures of the dark with "that peculiar / affirmative" yes: "a sharp, indrawn breath, / half groan, half acceptance, / that means 'Life's like that. / We know *it* (also death).'" *Yes*—I would draw my breath in while pronouncing it, like the Finnish *joo*. (I taught in Finland for a year and had learned the trick of that quiet gasp.) I was teaching the poem regularly by then, and what was at stake in that word had finally become clear. *Yes* was a taking in, an act of consent, the body's way of knowing. It was the body, in its breathy fragility, grasping the soul, letting itself go.

TOOLS

My favorite ellipsis comes near the end of Bishop's "At the Fishhouses." The poem opens with a long description repeatedly contrasting human tools (nets, shuttles, lobster pots, capstans, knives) with natural elements (the sun, sea, cold, the dark) slowly wearing them away. The "five fishhouses" of the title, with their firm, "steeply peaked roofs / and narrow, cleated gangplanks," seem at first to not fit this opening pattern, until you realize that they are in fact the same structures referred to later in that description as "small old buildings with an emerald moss / growing on their shoreward walls," seemingly eroded by the "heavy," "opaque" silver of the sea to an "apparent translucence." Bishop's title points us to this deliberate revision, as if description itself were another tool with which to approach the heavy, swelling sea, and the poet, just as clearly as the fisherman covered with the scales of countless fish, had felt the sea's weight and recorded its presence, her words eroded and reworked by what they couldn't hold.

This is an extraordinary moment—her body, in the face of the swelling sea and the darkening air, testifying, in taking its words back, to the weight of glory pressing down. The Hebrew *kabod* seems to exactly capture what she experienced there: glory as a "weight" pressing down, as, backwards to description, we turn back to the poem and continue on.

EDGE

Once the body comes into play, it continues to be engaged. The next stanza of "At the Fishhouses" picks up the thread, the poem moving from the fisherman repairing his net at the water's edge to the unmasterable sea itself:

> Down at the water's edge, at the place
> where they haul up the boats, up the
> long ramp
> descending into the water, thin silver
> tree trunks are laid horizontally
> across the gray stones, down and down
> at intervals of four or five feet.

And here we're forced to slow down again. We are staring at a ramp where boats are hauled up and lowered down, but it's not our minds that are engaged as we work our way through this sentence. Under the pressure of the overwhelming sea, desperate to enter but aware of its impossibility, it's our vulnerable bodies that "do" these lines. The eye looks "*down* at the water's edge" "where they haul *up* the boats, *up* the long ramp / *descending* into the water." This isn't information to be taken in. It's something our bodies do, our eyes moving up and down, wrestling ever more deeply with the drive to enter and the equally powerful drive to draw back. We're drawn down and down, but we have only these words to work with.

Which brings us to that ellipsis:

> Cold dark deep and absolutely clear,
> element bearable to no mortal,
> to fish and to seals . . .

And here the beautiful words break off, as if the poet has turned to the deepest language she has at her disposal (*cold*, *dark*, *deep*) and the lyric tradition behind them has given way. We are sitting with Sylvie in the dark as the walls of the house dissolve and the "unbearable" sea rises up to meet us. And then thrillingly, casually, in the space of that ellipsis, Bishop gathers up the shards of language tumbled into bits by the sea and moves on with them into the vertiginous space, saying yes to what she finds there—hear the intake of breath?—with that arms-wide acknowledgment of the body's vulnerability we call a joke:

> One seal particularly
> I have seen here evening after evening.
> He was curious about me. He was inter-
> ested in music;
> like me a believer in total immersion,
> so I used to sing him Baptist hymns.
> I also sang "A Mighty Fortress Is Our God."
> He stood up in the water and regarded me
> steadily, moving his head a little.
> Then he would disappear, then suddenly
> emerge
> almost in the same spot, with a sort of shrug
> as if it were against his better judgment.
> Cold dark deep and absolutely clear,
> the clear gray icy water . . .

This is for me more expressive than the resonant, deeply to be desired language Bishop had first turned to the sea with. It is the moment the poem had been written toward, the moment of our deepest engagement. Baptists of course baptize by immersion, and since Bishop and the seal are both believers, she sings him Baptist hymns, sounding out her deepest desire while also brushing it off as a joke, pretending she hadn't said any such thing and thereby uttering what couldn't be uttered. And we understand, because language has been at issue for us as well. We have found its limits within ourselves. The sea has eroded our words and given them back to us bent and broken, flexible and free. She sings to the seal, at home in its depths, and we follow her down, believers all, having taken these steps with her. I wish I had pointed my "backwards" student here. Bishop's joke would have been something we could share between us, "dot, dot, dot" a kind of quiet signal we might have exchanged, testimony that we had survived the ordinary giving way and plunging us into the new.

DISTRESS

It's not only language or description that comes undone. The body's fragility comes into play in multiple ways. Many springs, I would begin the semester with Hass's "The Apple Trees at Olema," a poem that explores this. Its first lines focus on a couple who are "walking in the woods along the coast / and in a grassy meadow, wasting, they come upon / two old neglected apple trees." The floating adjective *wasting* applies most directly to the untended meadow, but it also hovers over the trees and the couple as well. It's our first sense of the speaker's uneasiness about the story he's telling. The poem then shifts into past tense, a barely noticed, backwards-turning hesitation, in which the speaker loops back and attempts to tamp down the charged tension he's just introduced. It's a mark of vulnerability, this moving in and out of the present, much like Bishop's eye shifting up and down at the sea's edge. The limbs of the trees, he remembers, "looked rotten." They were covered with moss, but at the same time were "wild with blossom," and a "green fire / of small new leaves flickered even on the deadest branches."

From here, the speaker shifts even further back, to the moment the couple entered the meadow, before they caught sight of the trees, when, busying themselves with naming the wildflowers they discovered there, they had disagreed about "an intricate, leopard-spotted / leaf-green flower whose name they didn't know," he identifying it as "trout lily," she as "adder's-tongue." It wasn't until I looked up the names that I saw why the poem had turned back to this moment. Both are names for the same flower—the dogtooth violet—suggesting that none of these names is completely stable. Setting this issue in play puts the poet backwards to the very language he is using and prepares him, and us, to look more closely at the tension between the lovers' bodies, which he returns to now in the present tense, on high alert. About those trees:

> She is shaken by the raw, white,
>   backlit flaring
> of the apple blossoms. He is exultant,
> as if something he felt were verified,
> and looks to her to mirror his response.

Two bodies, with two different ways of responding, engage this open space, and we are called to work through each in turn. (The closest moment I know to this is Frost's "Home Burial," where the fragile difference between the way a husband and wife move through loss shakes the reader to the core.) She is taken aback by the sudden raw flare of color. He is exultant, as if he had found himself reflected there, and looks to her for confirmation. We all understand this problem, as does the speaker, who quietly comments, in a first-person, parenthetical introduction of another seam or stutter:

If it is afternoon, a thin moon of my own
    dismay
fades like a scar in the sky to the east of them.

I always needed to reposition myself in order to feel my way into this space between them, which the speaker does as well, returning to "he" and "she" after suggesting that of course there's been an implied "you" and "I" all along. This is the swamp we're moving through now, and it is within the body's understanding of difference that we join the poem in negotiating its space. She is shaken, he is exultant, and the poem slows to take that in. Looking for confirmation, he finds himself "knocking wildly at a closed door / in a dream" while she, behind that closed door, pondering her initial response, concludes that "it was the repetitive torn flesh / of appetite in the cold white blossoms / that had startled her," which frees her to look again:

                                        Now they seem tender
and where she was repelled she takes the
    measure
of the trees and lets them in.

But, as of course we had anticipated, in that brief pause, what had flared in him fizzles out, and "he no longer has the apple trees." Two bodies, with two ways of moving—as we worked this out in class, we would at some point pause and laugh at ourselves, acknowledging the inevitable and then move forward again, taking on the full terrible speed of desire.

CENTER OF THE MIND

This charged space between was "as sad or happy / as the tide, going out or coming in, at sunset," Hass continues, nodding to the inevitable but, in taking note of the sunset, offering himself a way to continue on. The couple, in separate spheres, turn to each other and notice, in the "flashing dull gold" of a lesser finch, a reflection of the sunset light in the rising spray of the reef below them. "They admire the bird together, / it draws them closer, and they start to walk again."

This deliberate action is a way of making a home in homelessness; Bishop's seal joke was another. This is the space in which poetry does its work, as Hass explains:

A small boy wanders corridors of a hotel
that way.
Behind one door, a maid. Behind another
one, a man
in striped pajamas shaving. He holds
the number
of his room close to the center of his mind
gravely and delicately, as if it were the key,
and then he wanders among strangers all
he wants.

The room number, of course, is no protection at all, and yet holding that number in his mind "as if it were the key" allows the boy to wander, attentively, through an immensity he could never think of mastering. A strangeness. That room number is a made thing, a renaming of the world after a blizzard. As Hass notes quite explicitly, it is an *as if*. It desires without imagining it could ever fully have. It is held in the mind, as a student once described our work in class, "gravely and delicately," a way of wandering in which danger is both acknowledged and embraced.

Hass was surely thinking here of Stevens. The boy holding his room number "close to the center of his mind" is a version of the poet whispering to the ear of the mind just what it wants to hear. Which is what? That, like this couple, the soul can find a home within our endless reaching, that the shared vulnerability we offer each other, each time we break the silence, grounds, without guaranteeing, the most intimate acts of speech.

TEMPTATION

I've been talking with a friend in philosophy who is interested in Wittgenstein's claim that "one should write philosophy only as one writes a poem." Perhaps twenty years ago, I had taken Jim's Wittgenstein class, having fallen in love with the sound of the philosopher's sentences and recognizing the uncertain spaces he was attempting to find his way through. I was in over my head in the class though, treasuring fragments of the writing but never sure of my footing. It was a start, however, and Jim and I became friends. We would get together and talk about what we were working on, and at some point I sketched the idea I'm developing here, that when we read poems we are called to reenact an inner movement, drawn not into a poet's illustration of a thought already arrived at but into their engagement with the pressures arising as we think or describe or remember or love. Jim saw Wittgenstein's focus on "what we want to say" in these situations, walking us through the temptations and gaps in understanding made visible in their vertiginous reaches, as a similar attempt to draw readers into the experience of "finding the path from error to truth" for themselves, an experience they could then carry out into the world. That is what writing philosophy as one writes a poem must mean —Wittgenstein seating himself backwards to the pictures that had held him captive and calling the reader to join him there, lost and accountable, engaging in the work of the spirit, finding a new way home.

IGNORANT

One of the poems Jim and I talked about was Bishop's "The Armadillo," set in Brazil, the poet describing a St. John's Day custom of launching "frail, illegal fire balloons" into the night sky. As the balloons rise and move away from us, they appear increasingly pretty, increasingly benign. They look like planets or stars or hearts. Bishop makes us feel, as we join her there, the tempting way distance seduces us and allows us to feel secure. Even when she draws back and describes the aftereffect of one of those balloons falling "behind the house," distance is still a part of how she sees. She focuses on three sets of creatures affected by the resulting fire, and in each account a careful distance grounds her vision. A pair of owls, their nest destroyed, is "stained bright pink underneath" as they rise, shrieking, above its flames; a glistening armadillo, fleeing the scene, is "rose-flecked" in the reflected light; and a baby rabbit, "a handful of intangible ash," echoes back the fire one more time with its "fixed, ignited eyes." This is a safe sort of empathy, the kind of thinking we are "tempted, seduced, bewitched, or dazzled by," as Jim wrote about Wittgenstein.

In order to "do" this poem, we have to imagine for ourselves the delicate play of reflected light across the inhabitants of this scene and then recognize the aestheticizing temptation we succumbed to. We have to feel beauty's power and be seduced by it. Slow down, I'd sometimes say. What did you see in that "handful of intangible ash"? A burning bunny? A wry laugh, because of course some of us had. No, what we saw was the hand of the writer, with our concurrence, brilliantly, "intangibly," balancing the rabbit's gray fur against the fire's ash. Which means, in the stanza break that follows, that when Bishop catches herself and recognizes what she's done, we too are indicted and then thrown backwards to our feelings of mastery, our eyes fixed on the picture that had held us captive. In its erasure, we are suddenly, disorientingly, set free. This must be what the soul wants to hear—that within our unseeing a space still exists in which inwardness might find a way to truth:

> *Too pretty, dreamlike mimicry!*
> *O falling fire and piercing cry*
> *and panic, and a weak mailed fist*
> *clenched ignorant against the sky!*

And what sort of truth is this? That we live in a world we cannot control. That we are creatures with bodies and not just minds, surrounded by fire, cries, and panic. We had been taken in by this world's "dreamlike mimicry" and then had been set free.

How might we then speak? Like this, the poem suggests in these final, italicized lines, approximating in the body what can't be said directly, raising fists in protest that are, at the same time, the armadillo's profile held against the sky—"mailed," "ignorant," vulnerable and exposed. This is language unstrung, an impossible joke, but surely no joke at all. Working through temptation, feeling it take hold and then crumble away, changes us as it has changed the writer. It sets us on a new path, embracing what can never be controlled.

SACRIFICE

I had a student once who hung wanted posters of me on my office door, in the classroom we met in, and on bulletin boards near the entrance to our building. My face, behind bars. I don't think the poster said "Dead or Alive," though I sometimes catch myself remembering it that way. We had been doing a series of poems, exploring these vertiginous spaces, and I imagined that this student had wanted to silence certain thoughts by locking me away, as if I was responsible for opening up something dark within. Which I suppose I was. It caused quite a stir.

In "The Tollund Man," Seamus Heaney describes a photo he'd seen of an ancient, preserved body discovered in the bogs of Northern Germany. Finding his way to what the photo stirred in him, he imagines driving through the area in which the body had been found and experiencing "something of his sad freedom / As he rode the tumbril" on his way to ritual sacrifice, the poet imagining himself

> Watching the pointing hands
> Of country people,
> Not knowing their tongue.
>
> Out here in Jutland
> In the old man-killing parishes
> I will feel lost,
> Unhappy and at home.

I felt like that that morning—tongues clucking, hands pointing, uneasy interviews with various authorities—as if I were riding that tumbril.

But I see that there was more to it. Heaney was trying to imagine violence-soaked Ireland being brought back to life, and he sensed that his own lostness might be a doorway, an intuition brilliantly realized three years later in "Punishment," in which he acknowledges his own hypocrisy, standing silent when "betraying sisters / cauled in tar / wept by the railings," the poet exposing the barbarity of their treatment and recognizing in himself the attractions of such a "tribal, intimate revenge." Acknowledging the picture that had held him captive, he took his place on that tumbril, offering the reader his own struggles as illustrative sacrifice.

Perhaps that's what my student saw—that I was fighting through my own captivity, exposing before the public what I had too easily found myself wanting to say. I had gone there deliberately, unsure of where it would take me, and it had landed me in jail.

BUT NOW

But why go there in the first place? I'm not sure I've answered that question yet. Think of the way a runner prepares by breaking a race into smaller pieces and running portions of it over and over in practice—"repeats," they're called. I did five times a thousand meters on the track this morning, for example, reminding my body of what it would take to ride that line of effort.

Jorie Graham taught me something about this as well. We were talking about pictures that had held us captive, and she took me to William Carlos Williams's "Spring and All." Williams attempts to describe something he sees "by the road to the contagious hospital," but his focus is immediately disrupted by the "surge of the blue / mottled clouds" above him and then by the "waste of broad, muddy fields beyond" that the clouds carry him out to. Find those "patches of standing water" out there, Graham told me, that "scattering of tall trees," and then pull yourself, as Williams does, back to the road and the "reddish / purplish, forked, upstanding, twiggy / stuff of bushes and small trees" along it, and only then, with him, return to the grass that first caught your eye, barely there, "lifeless in appearance," as "sluggish / dazed spring approaches."

What we feel in this arc is desire pushing our bodies out and beyond when nothing at hand satisfies. The poem pauses here for a moment, but then it begins racing again, leaping forward in time, still in the grip of desire: "Now the grass, tomorrow / the stiff curl of wildcarrot leaf / One by one objects are defined— / It quickens: clarity, outline of leaf," everything we had been wishing for. And here she grabbed my arm, almost in horror at what she'd seen in herself, that simple "now" by the side of the road disappearing in this returning, still hungry, reaching for more. She grabbed my arm and spun us around, backwards to what had been driving us, acknowledging our complicity: "But now the stark dignity of / entrance." It's that grip on my arm I remember—"*But now*"—desire checked and coming up short, as if one could actually experience what it felt like to be lost within its reaches. As if two of us were needed to stand against its surge, regaining the world as if it were lost, as if there were a line we could learn to ride, if we learned to ride it together.

FALL

I've always loved the moment in *King Lear* when Edgar leads his blinded father, Gloucester, to the edge of a nonexistent cliff in order to save him, using the space opened up by his blindness to teach him to see again. Gloucester wants to die. Edgar takes his hand, on the verge of what he describes as a terrible drop, and describes what he "sees" there, calling on his father to visualize the scene internally, much as we do when we read. "The crows and choughs" in the midway air seem the size of beetles. A gatherer of samphire, on the cliff below, "seems no bigger than his head." Fishermen on the beach look like mice, while an anchored barque looks like a towed rowboat. The waves surge but they can't be heard. As he unfolds the imaginary space Gloucester is about to fall through, Edgar guides him through its renunciation, having him measure it with his body and then let it go. Gloucester falls and faints, only to be brought back to consciousness by Edgar, in yet another voice, describing the many fathoms of his supposed fall and insisting that "thy life's a miracle."

Why take him through this? Why do something not unlike it week after week in class? Edgar tells us in an aside that he "trifle[s] thus with his despair" in order "to cure it." Gloucester has turned his back on the world, having seen its wonders come to nothing in the grip of his self-absorbed blindness, and falls through that vertiginous acknowledgment. Edgar lets him experience the loss of the world and then offers it back to him as a gift. There's of course a risk in such a path to truth. Edgar understood this, leading his father to this blindingly dark place and then standing aside as it carried him down. That long moment, before the world comes rushing back—I'm still thinking of my student, backwards to his body

—perhaps none of us would choose to go there on our own. But the gain—to rise with Gloucester as he regains his feet, rocking quietly in the bite of the air, to see, with him, in his blindness, "feelingly"—that, I'm convinced, is worth it.

CAPTIVE

I would call this spiritual work. Take Graham's "Two Paintings by Gustav Klimt." She begins with Klimt's painting of a beech forest, *Buchenwald*, unfolding, in herself, a deep response to its perfect, glittering stability and giving voice to a kind of impassioned moral yearning it stirs up in her. The dead, she writes, "in their sheer / open parenthesis," what wouldn't they give for something this solid "to lean on," for boundaries this clearly defined, "right and wrong like pools / of shadow / and light you can step in / and out of / crossing this yellow beech forest, / this *buchen-wald*." A pause, generated by the German *buchen-wald*, brings the poem to a halt, and Graham begins to study this initial picture. The blue air of the painting seems to "poke" at the glittering, yellow trees, prodding her to do the same.

"Why be afraid?" she asks herself, turning to a second Klimt painting in which the impulse she has just acknowledged in herself has quite literally come undone. The painter died suddenly while working on it, inadvertently revealing what lay behind the first painting's glittering, solidly defined surfaces. The woman's body Klimt had been painting was "open at its point of / entry, / rendered in graphic, / pornographic, // detail," the "scream / between her legs" not yet fully painted over with his "trademark" delicate garment. It takes a moment for this to settle in, and then Graham quietly confronts what this second painting has shown about our desire for stability and structure and clear demarcations of right and wrong. She is Klimt's invisible audience, as we are hers, having recognized in her own love for his beautiful surfaces a desire so deep it is willing to exploit and abuse and exterminate in order to get what it wants. That first "story" had captivated her,

its blues
and yellows glittering
like a stand

of beech trees late
one afternoon
in Germany, in fall.
It is called
Buchenwald, it is
1890.

Shaken, as we are doing the poem along with her, she considers the painting's 1890 title, linking its *Buchenwald* to the future death camp in some sense lurking under its seductive surfaces, and, in that motion, turns her back on its beauty and falls.

Or not—this is one of the great ambiguities of this poem, and contemplating it pulls our feet out from under us one more time—for the very dream of order and stability that Graham turns her back on is of course the same dream that has driven this beautiful poem and drawn us in. We are complicit, and in recognizing this we put our own selves behind its bars, beauty a picture continuing to hold us captive.

WIND

In *Moby-Dick*, Ishmael describes steering the *Pequod* one night, peering through the "red hell" of the tryworks and "yielding," in a kind of half sleep, to that same barbaric frenzy in himself. He drowses off and awakens in utter darkness—no light, no compass, and the horrifying sense that the ship is no longer bound toward a "haven" ahead but is instead "rushing from all havens astern." In the midst of this dizzying plunge, he realizes that he had turned backwards in his sleep and, hand still on the helm, had nearly capsized the ship. He turns about and rights the ship, but what's fascinating is what surfaces within him. That backwards plunge both breaks him free of the fires within—greed, hunger, violence, desire—and offers up their elements to think with.

This is the space poetry calls us to. "Look not too long in the face of the fire," Ishmael begins. "Believe not the artificial fire, when its redness makes all things look ghastly." In staring too long into the fire, he had "wander[ed] out of the way of understanding" and found himself in "the congregation of the dead," having turned his back on the living. Visualizing that backwards turn breaks the fire's hold over him and opens up a space in which, like "a Catskill eagle," he finds himself free to "dive down into [its] blackest gorges, and soar out of them again." He rights himself and comes about. He is on "the way of understanding," a path that will, in time, become *Moby-Dick* itself in all its improvisatory glory, looking back over the voyage, diving down into its fiery hells and soaring imaginatively up to the world's "invisible" heights.

In one of his poems from *This Clumsy Living*, my friend Bob Hicok describes a man writing a poem the day his wife dies, which doesn't surprise Hicok, since he too has "a mind that only lived / in his hands," making sense of a world as it rushes away by continuing to reach toward it. "Every time I write," Hicok continues, "I try to hold / the world still by noticing how the world moves." That would be poetry's "way of understanding"—embracing the moving world as it slips away, and in that failure, turning right to a wind in which spirit moves as it will.

CHOICE

There is something compelling about the moment when the picture we had trusted in comes undone. That may be why we come to poetry in the first place: the sense that here, finally, the veil has been lifted. But another danger lurks, which Graham helped me confront. I'm thinking of her poem "Fission," an account of where she was when she learned that Kennedy had been shot. I was eleven. She was thirteen, in a theater in Rome, watching Kubrick's *Lolita* with her father. She remembers in the poem the houselights coming on, the sound being cut, a man running down the aisle trying to get the audience's attention, and the now whited-out movie continuing to play in the background. She remembers, at that moment, Lolita confronting, over her heart-shaped shades, Humbert Humbert and everything that would follow. As did the young Graham, taking in the dawning of adulthood with her own body, the sound off, the lights on, "the magic forearm" of "the screen-building light" beginning to fray. The forward motion, the picture that, up until this moment, had held Graham captive, begins to come undone, "some likeness in it but not particulate." She remembers her thirteen-year-old self, now backwards to her body, "the story playing / all over my face my / forwardness," the theater lights touching her back and sides, the light from the now-open skylight touching the top of her head, "undressing something there where my / body is / though not my body."

This undoing brings her to a kind of "immobilism," a "being-in-place more alive than the being," in which, she now sees as an adult, she didn't yet have to choose—"*choice* the thing that wrecks the sensuous here the glorious here." "Don't move, don't // wreck the shroud, don't move," she tells the earlier self, responding, in a sense, to her thinking as she thinks. That freedom is compelling, but it's also its own kind of death if held on to too long, its own cage or shroud or set of bars. That would be the danger of this way of thinking, the inclination to stay undone forever. You can step away from adulthood and the body, and maybe you have to in order to see, but you can't stay there. You need to move again, out into the world, charged and vulnerable—we all do, our shared undoing playing across us, even as we leave the poem behind.

SIZE

Hass gave me some help in approaching this open-endedness. I remember our younger daughter, after her life had yawned open in front of her, spending hours in her room shifting around what she called her "little things," turning wrappers, sea glass, and bits of paper into temporary scaffoldings over the open space she found herself in, building and rebuilding them over and over, as if their constant circulation was in itself calming. Teaching was like that for me at first. My temptation was to keep our words in play, but I found in Hass another way of handling the sometimes unsettling observations my students would offer.

In "Santa Barbara Road," Hass creates what he calls "household verses," phrases and postures arising from the undoing of his marriage, which, delicately rearranged, draw our attention back to the marriage's fragile intimacies, lighting them up again from within. We were creating, in a sense, our own classroom verses. In one section of "Santa Barbara Road," Hass's three-year-old daughter Kristin identifies herself as "Mommy, Daddy, Leif" after the rubber duck that her father holds in his hand as he bathes her repeatedly insists she tell him who she really is: "Kristin's [just] a name." Her improvised response is a deeply true, deeply fragile renaming of herself as a delicate web of relationships, an arrangement seemingly pulled out of the air and taking one's breath away. Sometimes in the classroom, when all I could do was repeat what had just been said, a simple revoicing, I found myself leaning on Hass's memory of his daughter's words, drawing out a fragility none of us had yet taken in.

A similar sort of revoicing occurs in Hass's "Museum" when the poet notes that a couple in a museum restaurant—improvising, in half sleep, a circulating, "equitable arrangement" of baby, coffee, newspaper, and fruit—are surrounded by "faces carved in wood who are suffering the numbest kinds of pain: hunger, helpless terror." The couple takes no notice of what surrounds them, and yet, in the poet's juxtaposition, they seem to unknowingly push back one corner of that numbed darkness and shine a trembling light on it. Here again it is the poet —and I want to say, following his lead, the teacher—who draws out the fragile power of their testimony by taking it in through his own sense of fragility, in a sense cocreating their insight.

Hass describes this, in another poem, as seeing the world with your "eyes open," pushing back against its loss with what amounts to an act of faith, however fragile and torn and ultimately impossible to sustain that gesture might be: "What kept you awake was a feeling that everything in the world has its own size, that if you found its size among the swellings and diminishings it would be calm and shine." This would be what brought us to the classroom, morning after sleepy morning: the belief that everything had its size, and that together, even as it was torn from our grip, we might find a way to take its measure.

WEIGHT

I loved doing this together. When I was in grad school my mentor Larry Dembo was diagnosed with Parkinson's. I'm not sure when, but eventually someone who worked with him explained it to me. In fact, she asked me—I had an office across the hall—to keep an eye out and, if I hadn't heard him moving about when I was ready to leave, to go over to his office door, knock, and go in. He would probably be frozen in his chair and would need to be lifted up, which would start him moving again. We would talk a bit about our work and that would be that. In time, word got around, and I would sometimes get a call from one of his friends who had found him frozen in his car, in the parking garage under our building. I remember taking his weight in my hands, the calmness of his waiting. I learned that Larry would tend to freeze in transitions—from standing to walking, passing through a doorway, parking a car, turning to check behind him—and what he needed was someone to take that next step with him.

One day I got an email from a student explaining that I'd gotten Claudia Rankine's "Yes, but," "Yes, and" distinction in *Citizen* wrong. She quietly listed each use of the two phrases and suggested that "Yes, but" is how we defend ourselves, explaining away wounding words or dismissive gestures through some sort of face-saving deflection. I do this all the time. I'd made the opposite point in class, and as soon as I read her email, the tangle I'd created came undone. "Yes, and," she continued, looks squarely at the wound and goes into the space it opens up, however painful. She got me moving again.

I took it as a gift when Larry would welcome me into that space. For all his brilliance, this is what I remember—taking that step together.

DIFFERENCE

That step took many forms. In "The Accident," Laura Kasischke writes about a student in a poetry class "who could not read" and the way it took her all semester "to understand what he was faking" because the others, "who / seemed to read, seemed / also not to understand." There was something different about him, Kasischke finally realized. "Not / understanding made *them* / angry, while / He kept raising His hand to give me / better, stranger answers to my questions."

I've had students whose responses were so untethered to the poem in front of us that it seemed they were simply flinging the poem back in strange accents, their observations so detached from what we were performing that they introduced a kind of unreadability into phrases or figures of speech that I had made my peace with years ago. Kasischke compares the strangeness of such answers to God's replies to Job's tormented queries:

> Consider daffodils.
> Consider cancer.
> Consider certain tiny lizards, and that
>
> long before
> anyone could count
> there was still math.

To our anguished "What's going on here, it doesn't make sense," God (as Kasischke quietly suggests by capitalizing the pronouns) raises "His hand" and replies, as he did to Job, "Daffodils," "tiny lizards"—a world of wonders raining down, their radiant incomprehensibility drawing us deeper and deeper into a lostness in which we might find ourselves, called there to see again.

NOT UNORDERED

Gertrude Stein's "A Carafe, that is a Blind Glass" makes much of the overflow that such accidental remarks unleash. Consider a carafe, she oddly replies in this short poem from *Tender Buttons* (reproduced in full below), when in fact what we had apparently asked about was reflection:

> A kind in glass and a cousin, a spectacle and nothing strange a single hurt color and an arrangement in a system to pointing. All this and not ordinary, not unordered in not resembling. The difference is spreading.

This could be one of the "better, stranger answers" Kasischke wrestles with, entangling us in the difference between a "looking glass" and a "blind glass" without ever naming that looking glass directly. We have to find that missing term within ourselves in order to make sense of the two different ways of tracking the spirit's motion that the poem proposes. A carafe, we could say, offers "a kind" of reflection in glass, a "cousin" to that of the looking glass. It reflects not by mirroring a scene back but by creating a "spectacle," its "single hurt color" (think of red wine against a white tablecloth) refocusing what's before us into "an arrangement in a system" related to, but not the same as, "pointing." The carafe makes sense of the world not by reflecting it back but by rearranging it, much like Stein's own words do with the language before us, undoing and reordering it into a form in which brokenness, its left-unspoken words, is part of its pointing.

Turning back to the world after having done this work, having found a way through it, however uncertainly, we take the world in as both open-ended and yet comprehensible, "not unordered in not resembling" anything we might have expected. The body's "single hurt color," its testimony to what we can never reach and never hold, seems to be part of this knowing. That's "not ordinary"—this sort of writing never is—but it's also "nothing strange," as anyone aware of their body also knows. Its "difference" lights the world before us, "spreading" and reenchanting.

LONGING

I've used the term *spiritual* for this work of diving and soaring and diving again, making a home alongside the poet in homelessness. The Canadian poet Tim Lilburn calls such work apophatic, "a knowing which is an un-knowing," the failure to comprehend generating an impoverished longing "that changes us," making us "permeable" and receptive to "what draws but cannot be said." Think of Marilynne Robinson's "attuned" house. Lilburn describes this way of knowing as a "going home," a "craning toward the beautiful" in which desire itself becomes, as we wander, our only "home in an essentially alien world." Undergoing it, taking on its beautiful stutter, is as much an act of faith as any of the more traditional forms faith might take because of the work it calls us to: entering, and being changed by, the charged unknown.

Take Bishop's "The End of March," for example, a poem not written from a conventional position of faith but deeply committed to inward change. It begins with the poet walking a beach on an inhospitable day, everything "withdrawn," "indrawn," "disrupted," or "inaudible." The speaker attempts to make music from within these limitations, comparing the large dog prints she and two friends are following to lion prints and imagining that the "lengths and lengths, endless, of wet white string" they encounter must inevitably lead to a kite, but she comes up empty in both cases—no lion, no kite. This failure, this wounded fall, opens out, after a stanza break, into an extraordinary recital of everything she longs for, everything she desires—her "proto-dream-house" further down the beach but "dubious," out of reach. She imagines herself retiring and "do[ing] nothing, / or nothing much, forever" there: reading, writing useless notes, setting spirit ablaze in a "lovely diaphanous blue flame."

"Perfect," she says, "but—impossible" to reach on such a day. She and her friends turn back, backwards to that dream, and discover the broken world no longer inaccessible but lit from within by desire. They have been changed by coming up short, as has the language of the poem, opening itself to the boundless through the broken attunements of the body.

Each of us, as we read, had to find a way of accounting for this turn. The sun comes out for a moment and the drab stones become multicolored, throwing out long shadows that seem to be "teasing the lion sun," "a sun who'd walked the beach the last low tide" and left behind "majestic paw-prints," and who "had batted a kite out of the sky to play with." This is the language of *as if*, of play, humming with possibility, reaching toward a beauty new in the moment, suddenly within reach. Each of us, as we found our own way through this poem, gave the spirit we found there a local habitation and a name.

VANISHING

Let's return one last time to Wallace Stevens and "The Idea of Order at Key West." The poet and a friend are walking along the ocean and hear a woman singing. Her song interacts with the sea without, he explains, either dominating or being dominated. He and his friend are the invisible audience to her singing, deeply moved, but when they try to identify the "spirit" rising up to meet them, they conclude that it is neither the "outer voice" of the sea and sky nor the inner voice of the woman's response that had drawn them in. It is, somehow, the two together, song and sea, combining to render "the sky acutest at its vanishing."

That's an extraordinary idea, and one that reoriented my life—that the fragility of voice, alongside the world, never fully expressing or mastering it, might render its beauty more acute by adding to it our vanishing. The most striking fact about the poem is that when the woman's singing ends and the two men turn back to Key West, they discover that they had been changed. With the work they had done now alive in their heads, the lights of the fishing boats, "arranging, deepening, enchanting [the] night," make the world more acute.

That turn back to Key West, changed: I was running along Poverty Creek a few weeks ago and came upon a woman and a large dog, thinking to squeeze by them with a quick hello. The woman called out my name and I stopped. It was as if she had been expecting me. She had been my student years before, and as soon as I heard her voice it all came back. She wanted me to know that although she had been a "bad" student, her life had turned around. I remembered her struggle to write about "The Idea of Order," I said, but I hadn't remembered it as a failure. It was simply a poem she wasn't ready for yet. Over the years, she told me, she had gradually learned to read the poem and the experience had changed her. She had carried the poem with her the entire time, like a backpacker's paperback, tearing out pages as she went along as she gradually found a way in. Odd the way she suddenly appeared, just as I was returning to these lines. Like Athena to Odysseus. I began to run again, wondering if she'd still be there if I turned and looked, or if she had been swept back into the clouds. In the same way, these stories here, fragments of days unexpectedly returned to, call out our names, speaking them back, Stevens writes, "in ghostlier demarcations, keener sounds." I didn't turn around. I didn't want to know.

VOICE

Two years ago, a friend of mine had me record the pieces from my book *Sundays* on an old analog recorder. He loved the warm sound of tape, and I loved the short films two of his students made with the recordings—my voice, shifting between inner and outer landscapes, at angles to their not-quite-parallel series of images and an unfolding musical background. It was fascinating how clear and resonant my voice sounded against those juxtaposed streams. It was as if I were pushing off from them, as if they were my body thinking, their inner textures braiding back and forth underneath my spoken words.

When my voice came back and I began to write poetry again after decades of silence,

I realized that I had learned to recognize that voice in the classroom, riding twin streams of body and breath, mine and others', past the limit of what could be said and discovering, in that play of voices, a language just to the side of speech. "I believe in you my soul," says Whitman, calling the soul back to the body. "Bless the Lord, O my soul," writes the psalmist David, giving expression to exactly that same belief.

What we were doing, all those years, was calling ourselves to ourselves. This rising chain of tears and jokes and pauses, what the ear of my mind has most wanted to hear—I believe in that voice as well, and I came to it in teaching.

WELCOME

Talking about my morning run was one way I had of bringing voice and body into the classroom and inviting my students to do the same. It wasn't a simple place to start. The run was already receding. I knew how little of it, rising with my body above my body, could ever find its way into words, and most mornings I would end up shaking my head at the impossibility of it all. My opening words felt more like a stripping away than a building up, but I needed to start somewhere. "There is no other sound / In the darkness but the sound of a man / Breathing," writes R. S. Thomas, "testing his faith / On emptiness," nailing it to an empty cross. Bishop tests herself in a similar way in "One Art," inviting what had been silent back into the poem—"(*Write* it!)"—and then pushing hard against it. Silence is an empty church.

I've been working on these entries for a year now, making my way back to the classroom and the almost unrecordable work we did there. I think of these entries as another attempt to begin, still a little flushed from the morning run, fingers tingling with the cold. My voice, at first, always sounded a little strange, but how else would it sound when silence loomed so large?

ARC

We ended the poetry play with Stevens's "A Postcard from the Volcano," his meditation on what we leave behind when we are gone. It's a little blue. "Bones," he suggests, picked up by children with no knowledge we ever existed. But there's something else, what Stevens calls "the look of things, . . . what we felt // At what we saw."

In the play, each member of the chorus developed a signature set of gestures that they turned to as they unfolded the poems, finding their own ways through. I remember the night during rehearsal when they each were asked to articulate some crucial turning point in their lives and then to find that moment in their bodies—how they used those gestures to think with from that time on. As the play ended, Leah turned to each member of the chorus, reflected those gestures back to them, and then dismissed them each from the stage. We felt her sense of loss as the stage emptied. Each of them turned to the audience, peered back for a moment, and then moved on. There is so little we leave behind. The play was dense enough that I worried about what people would take away. But Leah seemed not to care. She was in love with the chorus's gestures, carrying deep within what each of them felt at what they saw. I loved them too.

At the end of class, I would turn to the board and make a show of erasing in order not to face the radiance fading, listening to my students shift past behind me, their voices carrying down the hall. What became of all that work? "Children . . . will speak our speech and never know," Stevens writes, thinking of that silent speech carried inside, there beside us down through the meadow, turning with us to our barns. Voices in the hallway, Leah behind us on the stage. The spotlight on her dimming but the work continuing elsewhere. The rhythm of their voices, down the long hallway, arcing across the sky.

ACKNOWLEDGMENTS

My thanks to the following friends and colleagues who have worked through these things with me over the years: Fred Carlisle, Weston Cutter, Dan Gardner, Laura Gardner, Jorie Graham, Peter Graham, Bob Hicok, David Hopes, Kylie Johnson, Jim Klagge, Tiffany Kriner, Nancy Metz, Jamie Penven, Patty Raun, Esther Richey, Bob Siegle, G. C. Waldrep, Edward Weisband, Rachael Wennermark. Tupelo Press published earlier versions of several of these pieces in an online Reader's Guide to my *Poverty Creek Journal*, for which I am grateful. My thanks as well to Lisa Ann Cockrel at William B. Eerdmans and Victoria Jones for their careful work with this book.

Grateful acknowledgment is made for permission to quote from the following works:

Excerpts from “The Armadillo,” “At the Fishhouses,” “The Man-Moth,” and “Poem” by Elizabeth Bishop. From *Poems* by Elizabeth Bishop published by Chatto & Windus. Copyright The Alice H. Methfessel Trust, 2011. Reprinted by permission of The Random House Group Ltd.

Excerpts from “I felt a Funeral, in my Brain” and “I dwell in Possibility” from *The Poems of Emily Dickinson: Reading Edition*, ed. R. W. Franklin (The Belknap Press of Harvard University Press, 2005). Copyright 1998, 1999 by the President and Fellows of Harvard College. Copyright 1951, 1955 by the President and Fellows of Harvard College. Copyright renewed 1979, 1983 by the President and Fellows of Harvard College. Copyright 1914, 1918, 1919, 1924, 1929, 1930, 1932, 1935, 1937, 1942 by Martha Bianchi. Copyright 1952, 1957, 1958, 1963, 1965 by Mary L. Hampson. Used by permission. All rights reserved.

Excerpts from “Desert Places” by Robert Frost. From *The Poetry of Robert Frost* by Robert Frost published by Vintage Books.

Copyright 1969 Holt Rinehart and Winston, Inc. Extract reproduced by permission of The Random House Group Ltd.

Excerpt from "Two Paintings by Gustav Klimt" from *Erosion* by Jorie Graham. Copyright 1983 by Princeton University Press. Reprinted by permission of the publisher.

Excerpts from "The Apple Trees at Olema" from *Human Wishes* by Robert Hass. Copyright 1989 by Robert Hass. Used by permission of HarperCollins Publishers.

Excerpts from "The Tollund Man" by Seamus Heaney from *Wintering Out*. Copyright 1972 by Faber and Faber Ltd.

Excerpts from "The Accident" by Laura Kasischke from *The Infinitesimals*. Copyright 2014 by Laura Kasischke. Reprinted with the permission of The Permissions Company, LLC, on behalf of Copper Canyon Press, coppercanyonpress.org.

Excerpts from "Of Modern Poetry" copyright 1942 by Wallace Stevens, copyright renewed 1969 by Holly Stevens Stephenson, from *The Collected Poems of Wallace Stevens* by Wallace Stevens. Used by permission of

Alfred A. Knopf, an imprint of the Knopf Doubleday Publishing Group, a division of Penguin Random House LLC. And by permission of Faber and Faber Ltd.

NOTES

This list catalogs the poems, essays, and other sources I cite in each chapter of the book, arranged in order of appearance. Most of the poems are readily available online. See, for example, the excellent websites poetryfoundation.org and poets.org.

• **Preface:** Tim Lilburn, "The Ethical Significance of the Human Relationship to Place," *The Larger Conversation: Contemplation and Place*; Shane McCrae, "Field of Encounter: A Conversation with G. C. Waldrep," *Image* • **Act of Finding:** Wallace Stevens, "Of Modern Poetry" • **Chain:** Kenneth Burke, "Symbolic Action in a Poem by Keats," *A Grammar of Motives* • **Body:** Walt Whitman, "Song of Myself," section 5 •

Touch: Emily Dickinson, "I felt a Funeral, in my Brain" • **Dash:** Elizabeth Bishop, "Poem" • **Lost:** Henry David Thoreau, "The Village," *Walden*; Emily Dickinson, "I dwell in Possibility"; Robert Frost, "Directive" • **Note:** Wallace Stevens, "The Snow Man" • **Pause:** T. S. Eliot, "The Love Song of J. Alfred Prufrock" • **Permission:** Galatians 5:1 • **Hair:** Emily Dickinson, "I felt a Funeral, in my Brain" • **Changed:** Jorie Graham, "Prayer" • **Backwards:** Elizabeth Bishop, "The Man-Moth" • **Charged:** Robert Frost, "The Wood-Pile" • **Vulnerable:** Jorie Graham, "Vertigo" • **Slip:** Elizabeth Bishop, Letter to Anne Stevenson, January 8, 1964 • **Line:** Henry David Thoreau, "The Pond," *Walden* • **Hands:** Herman Melville, "A Squeeze of the Hand," *Moby-Dick* • **Morning:** Robert Hass, "July Notebook: The Birds," "Museum," "Santa Barbara Road"; Henry David Thoreau, "Where I Lived, and What I Lived For," *Walden* • **House:** Wallace Stevens, "A Postcard from the Volcano" • **As If:** Virginia Woolf, "The Lighthouse," chap. 5,

To the Lighthouse; Robert Hass, "Spring Drawing" • **Attuned:** Marilynne Robinson, *Housekeeping*, chap. 5 • **Spirit:** Marilynne Robinson, *Housekeeping*, chap. 1 • **Poise:** Robert Frost, "Birches," "The Wood-Pile" • **Plunge:** Robert Frost, "Design" • **Turn:** Robert Frost, "Desert Places" • **Yes:** Elizabeth Bishop, "The Moose" • **Tools:** Elizabeth Bishop, "At the Fishhouses" • **Distress:** Robert Hass, "The Apple Trees at Olema" • **Center of the Mind:** Robert Hass, "The Apple Trees at Olema" • **Temptation:** James Klagge, "Doing Philosophy as Poetry," *Wittgenstein's Artillery* • **Ignorant:** Elizabeth Bishop, "The Armadillo" • **Sacrifice:** Seamus Heaney, "The Tollund Man," "Punishment" • **But Now:** William Carlos Williams, "Spring and All" • **Fall:** William Shakespeare, *King Lear* 4.6 • **Captive:** Jorie Graham, "Two Paintings by Gustav Klimt" • **Wind:** Herman Melville, "The Try-Works," *Moby-Dick*; Bob Hicok, "Waiting for my foot to ring" • **Choice:** Jorie Graham, "Fission" • **Size:** Robert Hass,

"Santa Barbara Road," "Museum," "Tall Windows" • **Weight:** Claudia Rankine, "An unsettled feeling keeps the body front and center" • **Difference:** Laura Kasischke, "The Accident" • **Not Unordered:** Gertrude Stein, "A Carafe, that is a Blind Glass" • **Longing:** Tim Lilburn, *Going Home: Essays*; *Living in the World as if It Were Home*; Elizabeth Bishop, "The End of March"; William Shakespeare, *A Midsummer Night's Dream* 5.1.17 (Malcolm Guite, in *Faith, Hope, and Poetry*, uses this quotation in a similar way) • **Vanishing:** Wallace Stevens, "The Idea of Order at Key West" • **Voice:** Walt Whitman, "Song of Myself," section 5; Psalm 103:1 • **Welcome:** R. S. Thomas, "In Church"; Elizabeth Bishop, "One Art" • **Arc:** Wallace Stevens, "A Postcard from the Volcano"

ABOUT THE AUTHOR

Thomas Gardner is Alumni Distinguished Professor of English Emeritus at Virginia Tech. He has published six academic books on literary and theological questions, including *Lyric Theology: Art and the Doctrine of Creation*, *Regions of Unlikeness: Explaining Contemporary Poetry*, and *John in the Company of Poets: The Gospel in Literary Imagination*. His two most recent creative books are the lyric essay collections *Poverty Creek Journal* and *Sundays*. His honors include the William E. Wine teaching award from Virginia Tech, the Outstanding Faculty Award from the State Council of Higher Education for Virginia, and Guggenheim and Fulbright fellowships. He and his wife live in Blacksburg, Virginia, at the edge of the Jefferson National Forest.

Text set in Adobe Caslon, designed by
Carol Twombly

Cover design: Jody Langley
Book design: Lydia Christine Hall
Copyeditor: Victoria Jones
Project editor: Jennifer Hoffman
Acquiring editor: Lisa Ann Cockrel

Here Below champions ambitious books
that eschew binaries between the sacred and
profane. Learn more at herebelowbooks.com.